M000113515

"*I'm convinced this is the best way to read the Bible.*" Adam

"*I'm enjoying it so much more than I would have imagined!*" Asheritah

"*These past few months have been an incredible journey that God is taking me on. He is speaking to me like He hasn't in a long time. I am excited for the future like never before.*" Jim

"*The good news, however, is that I am reading God's Word every single day. Something, I am sad to say, has not happened before in my Christian walk. I would read the Bible once in a while, but not daily. I need it. I am closer to God because of it.*" Ann

"*What a precious experience. Thank you. My relationship with the Word and The Author will never be the same!*" Beverly

"*The* Rapid Bible Read Thru *was the best way to kick start my new year. I am so glad I took on the challenge. It immersed me in God's Word like never before.*" Debb

"*I'm doing the RBRT for the third time. Reading in big chunks enables me to see the big picture, to recognize the significance of something in terms of something else read earlier but recently enough to see the connection. I recommend it to people all the time!*" Jona

"*This helped me see Bible reading as spending time with the Creator of the universe. In the past, it had become a task to be done.*" Jim

"*When other RBRTs failed, this chronological RBRT was completed! This is my 4th year completing a RBRT. I highly suggest it!*" Tammy

"*Wow! Just WOW! Such an awesome experience!*" Marty

"*It was truly an exhilarating experience to fall in love with our Creator in a more intimate manner!*" Susan

"Reading the Bible is so exciting and it is so good to do it regularly. And doing it together with so many other people from different corners of the world with different backgrounds, just reminded me how much our God loves us and how much I want to love Him better. And what better way to love Him if not by learning from His Word." Natalija

"Although reading through the whole Bible sounds daunting, it's much simpler than you'd think. Joining a RBRT is a great way to make new friends, gain fresh insight, and be encouraged in your pursuit of God. Here's to the power of community!" Susanne

"I did the RBRT to challenge myself to read a larger volume of Scripture, to try reading chronologically and above all to grow in my relationship with God. It's been way beyond my expectations and I can hardly believe that I'm almost done. A challenge worth taking!" David

"The RBRT has been awesome for me! I have never been this motivated to stay on track with my reading program." Traci

"I've been a Christian nearly my entire life and have always studied the Bible, but this challenge has changed me! I feel like I understand God on a whole new level. It's like the blinders have been lifted off my eyes and I see God with a new perspective and hear Him with a new heart." Brittany

"The RBRT challenged me to read ALL of God's Word and I could not be more thankful. I know the major "stories" of the Bible, but reading all God has to say to me, and reading it in chronological order, was such a blessing. I will look forward to doing the RBRT every year from now on!" Bruce

"As I read and kept on reading, I noticed "bigger" themes come to light that I had never noticed just reading smaller portions of Scripture at a time." Michelle

"The RBRT is a wonderful experience! It is so helpful, as it gives you guidelines that help make the goal more attainable and not so overwhelming. Also, you have the opportunity to interact with others who are reading at the same pace you are and be able to discuss questions or thoughts." Tamara

"I love being a part of RBRT. The comments of others on the site and responses to my posts certainly increased my understanding of His Holy Word. The challenge of reading through the whole Bible seemed a bit daunting, but by reading through whole books at a time and reading them in conjunction with what was actually happening in Israel at the time enhanced exponentially my understanding of the context. I wholeheartedly enjoyed and learned from it and look forward to the next RBRT!" Elizabeth

"This was my first time doing RBRT and I have loved it. Doing the read through has helped me see more of the whole story. It has also helped me to see things that I have not really noticed before, and I have seen how God uses more than one writer to confirm what is written. I would highly recommend RBRT (especially chronologically) as a way of freshening up the way you see the Bible, of making it come alive and of opening your eyes to more of what it contains. I will be signing up again next year." Lyn

"The RBRT was amazing! I have read through the Bible a few times in a year, but there was something different reading through in just four months. I got so much more out of the Bible, and it really wasn't that hard!" Marty

"I've completed two RBRTs now and I look forward to making this an annual plan. The shorter term goal of four months, as opposed to reading through the Bible in a year, is a pace that keeps me focused and on track. Soaking in large chunks of Scripture, rather than smaller pieces, gives me a better grasp of God's story and how it is woven together through the pages of His Word." Lisa

Rapid Bible Read Thru

Transform Your Understanding and Love for God's Word

Keith Ferrin

Rapid Bible Read Thru
Copyright © Keith Ferrin, 2016
Published by Keith Ferrin Productions, LLC

ISBN: 978-0-97400232-3

Book Cover Design: Brian Gage, Pipe & Tabor, Vancouver, WA
Interior Design: Alane Pearce Professional Writing Services, LLC, Baltimore, MD

For information or to schedule author appearances contact Keith Ferrin:

KeithFerrin.com

info@KeithFerrin.com

THIS BOOK NEEDS TWO DEDICATIONS

FIRST...

This book is dedicated to Ron Frost. In the fall of 2009, you challenged me to read through the Bible in less than six months.. My life and ministry have been changed because I accepted your challenge. I am forever grateful.

SECOND...

This book is also dedicated to the hundreds of people who have participated with me in a *Rapid Bible Read Thru* (or several) over the years. Some of you sat face-to-face with me in coffee shops here in Seattle. Hundreds more from around the world inspire, encourage, and challenge me through email, our Facebook group, or on my blog. Your questions shaped the content of this book and your encouragement led to its completion. Thank you.

TABLE OF CONTENTS

FOREWORD

I met Keith in 2009 at a waterfront restaurant on Washington's
Puget Sound. I wasn't sure what to expect. A friend's email
assured me we would hit it off. Keith, she said, is a man captured
by God's Word "like you are." That intrigued me, so we got in touch
and arranged the meeting.

I wasn't disappointed.

Keith, as promised, was devoted to Bible reading and we hit it off
right away. You might ask, so what does it mean to be captured by the
Bible? My answer is: read Keith's book and find out!

What Keith and I—along with many others—have discovered is
God's attractiveness. More attractive, in fact, than any of us will ever
fully grasp. God the Father wants us to know and love Jesus, his Son.
And Jesus wants us to know and love his Father. The Spirit, in turn,
guided the hearts of Scripture writers to make this captivating God
accessible to us as the Bible.

And this is the secret of rapid Bible reading. The Bible offers us
more than information about God. It ultimately invites us to taste and
see God's goodness: to be exposed to his heart. So Christ's call for His
disciples to "abide in my word" wasn't a call to duty as much as a call
to delight in who He is.

Keith makes this very clear here: our bond with God will grow ever
stronger as we press into God's relational offering. And, as Keith also
reminds us, we are much more likely to succeed in our pursuit if we
have companions for the trip—reading partners who share with each
other along the way.

That has also been my experience. In the fifty years of my own
rapid Bible reading I've had dozens of reading companions. Again
and again I've watched lives change: placid Christians suddenly come
to life. There is no greater joy than to watch real spirituality suddenly
emerge from the cocoon of ordinary church life.

Keith's book – although very brief – offers more promise than may
first meet the eye. It isn't pretentious. Keith offers practical advice that
is intentionally simple and accessible. But it is certainly profound. It's
a book that offers a pathway to God—to experiencing his love—that
can surprise and transform any readers who venture ahead with an
appetite.

In the meantime I'm continuing my own habit of regular rapid Bible reading. I still read through the Bible two or three times a year. And I can promise you that it never gets old! How I bless Sam, the retired missionary who opened my own eyes to the adventure of rapid Bible reading when I was just eighteen and getting started.

Dive into what Keith offers here. He'll coach you to read the Bible with minds and hearts fully engaged. And the richness of knowing Jesus better than ever before will make the journey worthwhile!

Ron Frost
Barnabas International

INTRODUCTION

The Bible is a long book.
There. I said it.
When people find out I'm doing a *Rapid Bible Read Thru*, the response is typically something like…

> *No way. That's impossible!*
> *How many hours a day do you spend?*
> *I could never do that!*
> *Good for you. I should do that…someday.*

My answers are usually something like…

> *Actually, it's not only possible. It's easier than you might think.*
> *It doesn't take "hours."*
> *Yes, you can.*
> *How about starting today?*

The next section is devoted to answering the "Why?" question, so I will keep it very simple here in the introduction:

> *If you want to grow in your understanding of the Bible, awe of the Bible, and love for the Bible – and the Author who wrote it! – doing a* Rapid Bible Read Thru *will be one of the best decisions you ever make.*

More on that in a few pages.

Before getting any further, we should probably take a couple sentences to make sure we're on the same page. You might be asking yourself, "*What is a* Rapid Bible Read Thru?"

Here's the definition I use (and therefore, the definition as it's used in this book):

A Rapid Bible Read Thru *is any reading of the entire Bible completed in six months or less.*

I am writing this book because, each year since 2010, the *Rapid Bible Read Thru* has changed me – and hundreds of others. And each year, the successes, questions, and struggles are similar.

After seeing the similarities in both the transformation that occurs, as well as the questions about how to do or host a *Rapid Bible Read Thru*, I figured it was about time to put it all down in one place.

The book you are holding contains three sections answering three questions:

Why should I do a *Rapid Bible Read Thru*?
How do I do a *Rapid Bible Read Thru*?
How do I host a *Rapid Bible Read Thru*?

I am so glad you are reading this book! You are about to embark on a wonderful, life-giving, transformational – and fun! – journey.

It is an honor to be your tour guide.

Alongside,

Keith Ferrin

PART 1

WHY SHOULD I DO A *RAPID BIBLE READ THRU*?

MY STORY

This chapter and the next will focus entirely on answering the "Why" question. Each will take a slightly different approach. What you are about to read is *my* story. Why I started. How I have been impacted. Why I plan on doing a *Rapid Bible Read Thru* every year for the rest of my life.

The next one will lay out some of the practical benefits you will experience *when* (notice I didn't use the word *if*) you take the plunge and do a *Rapid Bible Read Thru*.

IT ALL STARTED WITH AN EMAIL

It was an October morning in 2009. I was reading my email and opened one from a woman who had attended one of my *Falling in Love with God's Word* workshops earlier in the fall.

She wrote about Ron Frost, a former interim pastor at her church who did this thing called a "Bible Read Through." She thought our love for and approach to the Bible was similar enough that we should meet. She included a link to his blog[1] – and this article[2] in particular.

Little did I know the impact what I was about
to read would have on me.

The short version:

Ron wrote of meeting Sam – a retired missionary who was planting a church in British Columbia. While helping construct the new church

---

1   *Ron Frost's blog can be found at SpreadingGoodness.org/*
2   *Ron's post about how he got started can be found at* *SpreadingGoodness.org/?page_id=3*

over the summer, Ron noticed Sam's knowledge, application, and love for the Bible was truly unique.

When he asked Sam how he knew the Bible so well, Sam simply said, "I just read my Bible. I try to read it two to three times a year."

Once he picked his jaw up off the floor, Ron decided to take the challenge. He has been doing the same thing ever since. And that was 1966!

After I finished reading the blog post, I did what any other fully-committed, guided-by-the-Spirit follower of Jesus would do. I tucked it away on the back burner of my brain for a few months. (wink)

But the nudge was there. And it wouldn't go away.

By the end of 2009, I knew I had to do take the challenge. What better time to begin than January 1st?

I decided on four months. It sounded challenging, without being overwhelming.

At our church's men's breakfast on the first Saturday of January, I asked if anyone wanted to join me. To my surprise – and delight – five guys said yes.

Tom, Bob, Doug, Dick, and Robert. The initial *Bible Read Thru Gang.*

We all came from very different backgrounds. Tom was a mortgage broker. Bob was a senior project manager at a large electrical firm. Doug was a pastor. Dick was a builder. Robert was retired.

However, we all had one thing in common: *None of us had ever read the Bible in less than a year.*

In fact, Robert came to the first Tuesday morning gathering apologetically confessing that he didn't own and had never read the Bible at all! Two days earlier, he had taken one of the paperback Bibles from the back table at church.

It was truly a life-changing four months for all of us.

We saw things we had never seen before. Long-standing questions were answered. Insights were gained. Time lines were established. Gaps were filled in.

To a person, every one of us said it was more beneficial – and easier – than we had expected it to be.

I was hooked. I knew this was going to be a lifelong habit. Every year since 2010, I have spent the first four months reading through the whole Bible. I always have a group I meet with in-person. It's been as many as eight and as few as one. Sometimes only men. Sometimes a mix of women and men.

A few years into it I invited my blog readers to join me.[3] Thinking I would get a dozen or so people to join me, I was blown away when about 120 people jumped on board! Every year since, there have been about 200 people from around the world who make the commitment and share their insights, questions, struggles, and triumphs in the private Facebook group. (More on that in Part 3.)

Each year I look forward to January through April. It is *Rapid Bible Read Thru* time. I absolutely love it!

Now, please don't hear what I am not saying. (You might want to read that twice.) I love studying a book of the Bible deeply, hanging out with one person in the Bible, or thoroughly examining a theme, truth, or promise found in the Bible.[4]

But there is something special about the *Rapid Bible Read Thru*. Every January I feel like I am visiting an old friend. It's comfortable. It's enjoyable. It's…well…*right*.

I can honestly say it gets more enjoyable every year. More and more dots get connected. More of it sticks with me. I feel more sure of my own faith and the reasons for it. I have a deeper appreciation, awe, and love for God's Living Word.

Most of all, I love Jesus more.

Come to think of it, even if loving Jesus was the only reason for doing the *Rapid Bible Read Thru*, I guess that would be plenty, wouldn't it?

---

3   I blog regularly at KeithFerrin.com.
4   After all, it would be weird if I didn't love doing book studies, since I've actually written a book about the impact and process of doing a book study!

More Than You Could Ask or Imagine

*Now to him who is able to do immeasurably more than all we
ask or imagine, according to his power that is at work within
us, to him be glory in the church and in Christ Jesus throughout
all generations, for ever and ever! Amen.*
Ephesians 3:20-21

Now you've heard my story. You know why I started the *Rapid
Bible Read Thru* and why I keep doing them. It is time to hear
why others do it.

The benefits in this chapter come primarily from the emails,
comments in the Facebook group, and in-person conversations with
the hundreds of people who have done a *Rapid Bible Read Thru*.
(Although I enthusiastically affirm having experienced these benefits
myself.)

If I only told you *my story* and why *I* think you should do a *Rapid
Bible Read Thru*, you might be tempted to write it off and say, "Well,
Keith is a 'Bible-guy.' He reads it all the time. Writes about it. Of
course, he's going to say it's a good idea."

But these four benefits (as well as many others) have been
experienced by hundreds of people who are teachers,
stay-at-home moms, college students, computer engineers, retirees,
accountants, and sales people.[1] Simply put: Anyone who does a *Rapid
Bible Read Thru* can and will experience these benefits.

---

1   *If you want to read what these people have to say with absolutely zero
commentary from me, simply check out the pages in between the cover and the
title page. I've pasted a bunch of them there.*

Benefit 1:
Deeper Love for God

This helped me see Bible reading as spending time with the Creator of the universe. In the past, it had become a task to be done. - Jim (2016 Rapid Bible Read Thru *participant)*

People talk frequently about loving God more, better, deeper [insert your favorite descriptive word here]. But how often do we take practical steps to make it happen?

Multiple times every year I get emails or read Facebook comments from people who say things very similar to what Jim said above.

Doing a *Rapid Bible Read Thru* is one of the absolute best ways to deepen your love for God.

It makes sense doesn't it? When you spend more time with someone, you typically appreciate them more. When you hear about someone's passions, frustrations, hopes, and promises, you feel connected in an increasingly intimate way.

Reading the Bible for 45-60 minutes may seem like a lot. But what if you thought about sitting in a coffee shop with one of your close friends for the same amount of time? My guess is the hour would fly by. In fact, you'd probably wish you had more time!

The flip side is also true. If you only spend 5-10 minutes with someone, once every few weeks, how deep would that relationship get? I'm going to go with "not very."

Let's continue looking at person-to-person, in-the-flesh relationships for a few more sentences. Think of someone you are really close to. Someone who is super easy to talk with. Someone who knows you well. Someone you love deeply.

Now, do you *always* have long conversations with that person? Probably not. I'm guessing there are many times when you touch base with a quick phone call or a text.

The longer conversations make the quick "check ins" more fun. When the relationship is already deep, a brief text, phone call, or 2-minute chat in the grocery store reinforces – and can even deepen – the relationship.

The same is true with God and His Word. If you only read it in "soundbites," you might be encouraged, learn something, or find the words comforting. However, those soundbites won't lead to a strong, intimate relationship.

On the other hand, when you read big chunks of the Bible and regularly hang out with Jesus for extended periods of time, the impact of the quick soundbite increases. When you run across a short word from the Bible (on the radio, in a book, on social media, etc.), they will be *more* fun, *more* inspiring, and *more* likely to deepen the relationship.

Benefit 2:
Deeper Appreciation for the Bible

"Oh, how I love your law! I meditate on it all day long."
-King David (Psalm 119:97)

Wouldn't you love to have King David's heart for the Bible? As you might imagine, I believe you can.

When it comes to appreciating, enjoying, and loving the Bible, the Number One contributor for me was when I started reading the Bible with a *relational* mindset – rather than an *informational* one.[2]

The Number Two contributor has been the *Rapid Bible Read Thru.*

Don't get me wrong. I love the details! I love studying a single verse – or even one single word – of Scripture. I love it *even more* now that I have read the whole Bible several times.

When you read the whole thing, you start to see the story. Themes stand out. Time lines make sense. You notice someone who shows up several chapters apart – or even in different books.[3]

You start to see how everything fits together. You see how each part of the Bible complements and reinforces other parts. You appreciate not only the message of the Bible, but the beauty of it.

The common amid the majestic. The uses of various styles of writing. The authors from different cultures, time periods, and educational backgrounds. Deep, theological truths, unpacked in countless ways.

All of it woven together by the Master Storyteller. Oh, how I love your law!

---

2   *I write and speak on relational Bible study more than any other topic. You can find out more at RelationalBibleStudy.com (or on my blog).*

3   *Check out Nicodemus in John 3, 7, and 19...or Andrew in John 1, 6, and 12...or Silas in Acts 15, II Cor. 1, and I Peter 5. I would have missed some very cool connections if I had stuck with the chapter-a-day method.*

BENEFIT 3:
DEEPER UNDERSTANDING OF GOD'S WORD

*"The only way you can be saturated with the thoughts of Christ
is to saturate yourself with the book that is all about Him."*
-John MacArthur (Author and Pastor)

This one is probably the most obvious of the four benefits. If you read more of anything – and you read it quickly – you will understand and retain more. If you read less – and spread it out over a long period of time – you will understand and retain less.

If you've ever heard me speak, you've probably heard me use the "movie analogy." The short version goes like this:

Watch the movie first. Then study the scenes.

Think of the last movie you watched that had lots of plot twists and turns. Could you imagine watching one scene a day over the course of a month or two? Yikes! There is no way you would make sense of it all.[4]

That said, if you watched the movie in one sitting, watching a single scene later on will be fun – and helpful.

Think of a *Rapid Bible Read Thru* as watching the movie. Or better yet, if each book of the Bible is a movie, think of it as watching a whole movie *series*. We all know people who watch every *Star Wars* movie straight through during the week – or in one, really long day – before a new episode is released.

They not only love the movies, but it's also a refresher of the characters, plot lines, and unfinished business from the previous movies.

I started the introduction by saying the Bible is a really long book. We all need a refresher. It keeps it clear in our heads, and provides the background for any other deep study we choose to do.

---

4   *If you've seen the movie "The Sixth Sense" you know exactly what I mean. If you haven't, I dare you to watch it one-scene-a-day and try to figure it out. Yeah…let me know how that goes.*

Benefit 4:
Deeper Relationships with your *Rapid Bible Read Thru* Group

*So encourage each other and help each other grow stronger in
faith, just as you are already doing." The Apostle Paul
(I Thessalonians 5:11, ESV)*

While the previous benefit might be the *most* obvious, this one is likely the *least* obvious. But it's a fantastic benefit!

Every year, the relationships I have with the people I'm doing the *Rapid Bible Read Thru* with are deepened. When we see each other in other settings – or even after the *Rapid Bible Read Thru* is completed – there is more to talk about.

And I don't mean just Bible topics. It is easier to talk about family, work, or life in general.

I mentioned that each of the last few years, I've invited my blog readers to join me and we created a private Facebook group. Something interesting happened during the very first year. And it's happened every year since.

People from different states, different generations, and different countries shared not only their insights and questions, but also their struggles and prayer requests. They prayed for each other. They connected outside of the group. They even maintained the group long after the *Rapid Bible Read Thru* came to an end.

Let me say that again: People from various walks of life *started* a relationship doing the *Rapid Bible Read Thru*. They *continued* the relationship long after the *Rapid Bible Read Thru* was over.

There is something intangibly powerful about relationships started – or strengthened – during intentional conversations centered on the Word of God.

Let's get to it!

Hopefully, you are excited. I know I am!

I want you to experience every one of these benefits. And I know you can…and will.

What if I told you that less than six months from now you could love God more deeply? You could appreciate the Bible more. You could understand the Bible better. You could experience deeper relationships?

Would you go for it? If so, keep reading. The rest of this book is devoted to showing you how.

PART 2

HOW DO I DO A RAPID BIBLE READ THRU?

START WELL
(SO YOU CAN FINISH WELL)

I would guess that starting a Bible Read Thru – no matter if it's at a rapid pace or spread out over a year – isn't the problem. Finishing. Now, that's another story.

By far, the most common response I get when the topic of a *Rapid Bible Read Thru* comes up is some form of this...

> *"I have started reading through the Bible a bunch of times. I always get busy...or bored. Since I've never even completed one in a year, I can't imagine how I could possibly complete one in less than six months!"*

How about you? Have you started one? Have you *finished?*

I want you to finish. I believe you can finish. I believe you will finish.

The next few pages will show you how to start in a way that makes finishing not just possible, but probable. We will look at four "preliminaries." I'm giving them their own chapter because they're not technically part of the process. That does *not* mean they aren't essential.

Think of it this way. Let's say you decided to run your first marathon. Having a day-by-day training plan is a must.

Things like buying a really good pair of running shoes, finding a training partner, and actually signing up for a race that's nine months down the line aren't technically part of the process. And yet, they will significantly increase your chance of success.

Think of these four preliminaries as your running shoes, training partner, and signature on the dotted line.

THE MINDSET

Just last night, I had a 20-something guy come up to me after an event where I was speaking. He asked me the same question I'm going to ask you now:

What is the main reason you read the Bible?

Pause and think about this for a minute (or twenty minutes). Why *do* you read the Bible? Is it to "get something out of it?" Is it to learn? Is it to apply God's truth to your life? Is it to find words of comfort?

My answer caught him off guard. I simply said, "I read the Bible to hang out with Jesus."

To be with Him. Learning, knowing, application and comfort certainly stem from that relationship. But they are not my primary purpose. The purpose is the relationship itself. This is important enough, I'm going to go ahead and give it an entire line all by itself...

The primary purpose for reading the Bible is relational...
not informational.

I have written and spoken a lot on the topic of relational Bible study[1], but it's worth taking another paragraph or two before we move on.

It is way too easy to slip into an informational mindset when reading the Bible. After all, God's got something to teach you every day, right? Wrong!

Many days he does, but not *every* day. Some days He simply wants to comfort you, or challenge your thinking, or give you a word for a friend, or – dare I say it – simply have you enjoy the read!

Just as I have days where I teach, discipline or comfort my own children, I also have days when I jump on our trampoline, go to a ballgame, or sit and watch a funny movie. Those days are not less valuable! (And might even be more valuable.)

As you start your *Rapid Bible Read Thru*, make sure you keep a relational mindset. Pray that God would help you. Remember: The goal is hang out with Jesus. You do not have to learn something every day. Some days, God simply wants you to enjoy the read. After all, the Bible isn't just <u>The</u> Good Book, it's also <u>A</u> good book.

---

1   *If you're interested in finding out more about a relational mindset, I've devoted an entire chapter to this in my book* How to Enjoy Reading Your Bible.

The Approach

One of the first things people do when they think about starting a *Rapid Bible Read Thru* is figure out how much they're going to have to read each day to complete it in a whatever timeframe they have chosen.

They do that by either dividing up the number of chapters in the whole Bible (1,189) or pages in their Bible (mine has 1,243) by the number of days they will be reading. Here's a handy chart so you don't get distracted looking for a calculator. And I rounded up since stopping in the middle of a chapter feels weird. (Or is that just me?)

Whole Bible	1 Month	2 Months	3 Months	4 Months	5 Months	6 Months
1189	40/day	20/day	13/day	10/day	8/day	7/day

Now that you've seen the chart – *forget about it.* Here is why.

If you pick a timeframe, look at the chart, and dive in, your brain will *always* say, "I've got XX more chapters to get through today." How's that for killing the relational mindset? Could you imagine sitting down for coffee with a friend and thinking "I've got three more questions to get through before I can be done with this conversation."[2]

The internal conversation needs to change if you're going to not only start, but finish the *Rapid Bible Read Thru*. You need the right approach. And it's not complicated. Quite the opposite actually.

Simply shift your approach from reading an amount of <u>content</u> to an amount of <u>time</u>.

That single shift in your approach will make a world of difference. The average chapter – read out loud at a normal rate of speed – takes

---

2   *Ok. Some of you have friends, or coworkers, or family members where you are thinking that exact sentence. I'm sorry and I feel your pain.*

about four minutes. So, if you've chosen six months, it's about 30 minutes of reading each day. If you've chosen four months (that's my default) it's about 40 minutes of reading.

My suggestion is to figure out about how much *time* you need to spend reading, and then read about 5-10 minutes longer than that each day. That way, *you will always be ahead.*

If you only read exactly enough to complete the *Rapid Bible Read Thru* in the exact amount of months you have chosen, you will not succeed. Period.

There *will* be days when you can't read the full amount. The kids – or you – will get sick. You will forget to set the alarm. You will have to catch an early flight. Life *will* happen.

Rather than kicking yourself for falling behind (which is another topic entirely on how we view God) and struggling to catch up, the next day you'll simply pick up where you left off and carry on.

A quick story about my very first *Rapid Bible Read Thru*. A few chapters ago I mentioned the five other guys who joined me. We all decided to set aside an hour a day, not thinking much about getting behind (or ahead for that matter).

The end result? The slowest of us finished a month early! And remember Robert, the retired guy who had never read the Bible? Well, he finished in 78 days!

Time trumps content every time when it comes to finishing – and enjoying it at the same time.

THE BIBLE

I'll make this one super simple: Use a physical Bible.

Yes, it might not be as convenient. Yes, you might like to take notes on your phone or tablet. Yes, we're living in the 21st Century.

Convenient does not necessarily mean effective.

Few things are more distracting than holding a device that can do a thousand things. Few things will help you focus more than holding something that can only do one.

A physical Bible won't receive a text. A physical Bible won't tempt you to check social media, quickly glance at an email, or jot down a task for tomorrow.

You might think putting your phone in Airplane Mode will help you focus. And it will. A little. But the temptation to do something, check something, or look up something will *always* be there. Always.

Grab a physical Bible. Sit down. And read. Just you, your Bible, and Jesus. (Sounds pretty nice, doesn't it?)

One last thing about choosing a Bible. I strongly (it's tempting to use bold, italics, and underlining here) recommend *not* using a study Bible. You know those notes at the bottom of the page? And the beautiful pictures of the cities, temples, and artifacts? And the helpful maps of Paul's journeys or the Israelites wandering in the desert?

They will distract you. They will beckon you to come hither down the page.[3] They will call to you like Java Chip ice cream calls to me.

Hear this: Study Bibles are fantastic. I love mine. I use it frequently. But I don't use it when I'm doing a *Rapid Bible Read Thru*. It's too tempting – and easy – to read one of the notes, only to realize you've just read *all* of the notes on the page and only read one chapter of the Bible.

Your best bet for success is to use a physical Bible with as few notes as possible.

THE LOCATION

I would say the first three preliminaries are nearly essential to a successful finish. This one is more in the category of "really helpful."

Pick a spot where you read every day.

Make it a spot where you don't frequently sit to do other activities. Not the spot where you normally sit while watching TV. Not the spot where you pay bills, eat your breakfast, or check social media.

Make this spot special. And prepare the spot the night before. Make sure your Bible is in place. Have your reading glasses there waiting for you. Take care of the distractions before you even start.

After all, you are about to spend time with the God of the Universe. Having a location free from distractions will help you be fully present.

He is fully present with us. Shouldn't we be fully present with Him?

---

3   *I've always wanted to use "come hither" in a book. Kind of fun. Not sure I'll do it again though.*

Keep the Process Simple

My prediction is you are going to get to the end of this chapter and say, "Wait! That's it? That's all there is to it?" My answer will be, "Yup."

You see, there is a myth going around. You will find it in corporate settings. You will find it in schools. You will find it in churches. And sadly, most of us buy into it.

What's the myth?

Helpful things are complicated.
Really helpful things are really complicated.

What's the truth?

Simple gets applied. Complicated gets set aside.

The actual process for doing a *Rapid Bible Read Thru* is simple. Really simple. In fact, there are only three guidelines.

Guideline 1: Commit to a Timeframe.

Sometimes we look at committing – especially to a timeframe – as a legalistic, freedom-squelching concept. I see it as practical.

Think of someone you know who accomplishes a lot. Ask them how they do it. Some form of goal-setting will have taken place. When productive people want to accomplish something challenging, they set goals. Then they commit to those goals.

Pick a timeframe between one month and six months. Then commit to it.

I know a couple people who have committed – usually with one other buddy – to read the whole Bible in less than a month. That would certainly have fantastic benefits, but you're probably going to need to rent a cabin, skip work, and ship the kids to grandma's house for a few weeks. If you can swing it, more power to you! If not, keep reading.

On the other end of the Bible-read-thru-spectrum, I have known lots people who have read through the Bible in a year. Many have enjoyed it immensely. Many have made it an annual habit. Many own a One-Year-Bible and they use it every day.

However, this is a *Rapid Bible Read Thru*. If you truly want to grasp the "Big Picture" of the Bible – and enjoy it at the same time – I believe a year is too long. Six months or less is where you need to be.

A few chapters ago I mentioned that I am *not* against the verse-by-verse, deep study of the Bible. (In fact, I am a huge advocate of in-depth Bible study.) But remember: A *Rapid Bible Read Thru* is about watching the movie. Verse-by-verse studying is about digging deep into the scenes of the movie. Both are valuable. Both are necessary. Both have different processes.

Before looking at *Guideline 2*, let me first say I have found that 4-6 months – rather than 1-3 months – is the best bet (at least the first time around) for a *Rapid Bible Read Thru*. For most people, it is a bit more than they are doing now without being too overwhelming.

You might be reading 10-15 minutes a day (or not at all). If so, go for 25-30 minutes and commit to five or six months. If you're already used to doing 20-30 minutes of Bible reading, challenge yourself to read 45-60 minutes a day for three or four months. You'll be glad you did.

GUIDELINE 2: GRAB A PEN

If you are someone who reads nothing but novels, this will be something new for you. If you are someone who loves to write down anything and everything, you'll need to tone it down a little.

The bottom line is you want to jot down what stands out to you, what you want to chat about with your partners (we'll get to them in a minute), or questions, topics, and people you want to explore more deeply at another time.

You will definitely need to adapt *Guideline 2* to personal preference. Some of you love to underline and color-code your Bible so much it looks like Noah's rainbow showed up on every page. Some of you wouldn't dream of marking up your Bible. Either way is fine. You simply need a way to capture those thoughts, insights, and questions.

If you are not going to take notes directly in your Bible, have a notepad nearby. I have included several blank pages for notes in the back of this book. You can keep track of the date of your *Rapid Bible Read Thru* as well as the folks who are joining you.

Personally, I like to use a digital notepad. I don't use my phone, but I have an old tablet that has very little on it (and definitely no social media). The beauty of the digital notebook is, even though I'm not taking notes on my phone, it *synchronizes* with the apps on my phone and my computer so I can find those notes anytime and anywhere. Lovely.

Make sure you don't overdo *Guideline 2*. It is really easy to do. It is easy to turn a quick note into a 600-word journal entry. Do that later. It is easy to tie the passage into a Sunday school lesson you will be teaching next weekend. It is easy to want to stop and write a blog post. (OK, maybe that one was just for me.)

This will take some figuring out and experimenting. I try to write no more than three or four notes a day. Some days I don't write any. Other days I jot down ten or more. Neither is "wrong" per se. You just want to make sure you aren't still in Genesis at the end of your third month.

GUIDELINE 3: FIND A FEW PARTNERS

You already know I had five partners for my first *Rapid Bible Read Thru*. I have had as many as eight and as few as one other guy.[1]

If you have a partner who is really committed, doing a *Rapid Bible Read Thru* with one other person is terrific. That said, I find that most of the time, asking three to five people to join you is typically best. That way, if someone is sick, oversleeps, or is out of town on business or vacation, the group still meets.

And that's the key. Make sure the group meets.

Part of committing is not just doing the reading, but showing up each week. It can be in a living room or a coffee shop. You could meet in a corner of the church while your kids are at youth group. You could go out to lunch after church for a few months. *Just make sure you meet.*

---

1   *If you include the Facebook groups I start each year, then that number jumps up to about 200. Here I am talking about "live-and-in-person" partners.*

Finding a few partners is, by far, the most neglected of the three guidelines. That's tragic. So many of the benefits from Part 1 of this book are discovered or deepened when the group gets together.

No matter how many times I get together with other people who are reading the Bible, I am *always* amazed by what they see that I missed. It is really cool to see someone's eyes light up as they share a conversation they had with God through His Word earlier in the week.

We have had so many fantastic, challenging, encouraging, and eye-opening conversations over the years. Simply put: You can't catch everything. I certainly know I can't.

There is also the "fun factor" of getting together. Think about *anything* you love. Don't you love it more when you can either do it or share it with someone else? Yes, there are some things you like to do alone. But every time? Probably not.

I love sports. And I don't mind watching sports alone from time to time. But if I could *only* watch sports alone? That would get pretty boring, pretty quickly.

You might be a painter who enjoys being in your studio alone. But I'm guessing you like to share your art with others, or tour a gallery with another art-loving friend. I have also known cooks who could spend hours alone in a kitchen. Typically, however, that cook's joy is increased greatly when they sit down to share what they've created with family or close friends.

God created us to be in community. And God created His Word to be read in community.

Commit to a timeframe.
Grab a pen.
Find a few partners.

You can adapt these guidelines. But you certainly don't want to leave any of them out.

You can choose to read for two months or six months. *But make sure you commit.*

Your pen might be a black ink, digital, or a pencil. *But make sure you grab it.*

You might choose to meet with one person, several guys, a few other students, or a another couple. *But make sure you do it together.*

That's it. I told you it was simple. Simple gets applied.

WHAT ARE THE MOST COMMON QUESTIONS ABOUT DOING A *RAPID BIBLE READ THRU*?

O ver the years, I have received heaps of questions via email, Facebook, and in person about doing a *Rapid Bible Read Thru*. Thinking I might one day write a book about it, I started keeping track of those questions. Once I actually decided to start writing, I sent a survey out to over 3000 people asking them what questions they have about doing a *Rapid Bible Read Thru* and what questions they have about hosting one.

I wanted to make sure I was creating as complete a resource as possible. I took the questions from the survey, combined them with the questions I had been compiling, looked for overlaps (there were a lot), and created the list that follows[1].

This chapter is more to be scanned than read straight through. Look through the questions and see if any of them match questions you have. As you get started with your reading, if you have a question, come back here and see if I have already answered it. If not, you can always reach out to me. Check out the "Let's Connect" page at the end of the book.

---

1   *This chapter is **only** the questions having to do with <u>doing</u> a* Rapid Bible Read Thru. *Questions about <u>hosting</u> can be found at the end of Part 3.*

HOW DO I STAY FOCUSED?

This is – by far – the most common question I get. So this answer will be a bit longer than the rest.

Sadly, the question of focusing is largely rooted in our *expectations* of the Bible. Most of us expect the Bible to be true, but we don't expect it to be enjoyable. We expect to learn something, but we don't expect to be engaged. [Insert heavy sigh here.]

Remember, we're talking about somewhere between 30-90 minutes a day. If I told you to sit down and read a novel for an hour each day, you might wonder where you'd find the time, but you certainly wouldn't ask about how to focus. You would focus because it would be enjoyable. You would expect it to be enjoyable…and it would be.

The feedback I have gotten is that, for most people, the simple act of reading more in each sitting helps them focus. It makes sense. After all, it lines up with how our brains are wired.

I heard about a study done on reading and focusing.[2] The study found that it takes most people about ten minutes to "turn off the voices" when they read.

When I heard that little nugget, a light bulb went off in my head. Most people never get to the 10-minute mark when they are reading their Bibles. Here are the three most common ways people read the Bible:

- Devotional book – The Bible reading in an average devotional will take you 30-60 seconds to read.

- Chapter-A-Day – The average chapter of the Bible, read out loud at a normal rate of speed, takes about four minutes.

- Bible-In-A-Year – The average daily reading is about 12 minutes.

Thirty seconds. Four minutes. Twelve minutes. Most people never come close to ten minutes. And the ones who do, stop immediately at the point where their brains would go into "storytelling mode" and they would begin to enjoy it!

One last thought on the question of focusing. Pray. A lot. The enemy doesn't want you to focus. He doesn't want you to enjoy God's Word. So he is going to attack. Especially in the first several weeks.

---

2   I've looked for this study and haven't been able to relocate it. If you find it, let me know and I'll reference it in future printings of this book.

Pray before you ever start reading. Pray that God would protect your mind, calm your mind, and engage your mind. Pray throughout the day that God would bring His Word to your mind as you are "along the road" (Deuteronomy 6). Pray for your partners. Pray in advance for the reading you will do tomorrow.

WHAT IS THE BEST TIME OF DAY?

The short answer is: Whatever time you can be *consistent*.

That said, I find that way more people (including myself) find consistency early in the morning. I have certainly talked to people who love to sit and read in the evening. A few moms have told me they use the hour immediately after dropping their kids at school. Other people take their lunch hour, head out to their car, and do their reading while they eat.

It all comes down to consistency. While different schedules provide different times where you can be consistent, I can count on one hand the number of people who have tried to "fit it in" each day and successfully completed a *Rapid Bible Read Thru* in six months (let alone fewer than six months).

WHAT TRANSLATIONS DO YOU RECOMMEND?

Let me just say, there are lots of good translations out there. You may have one you grew up with, your church uses, or has been recommended to you. Some people tell me they purposely grab a translation they are *not* as familiar with so they can read the Bible with fresh eyes. In any event, here are the four translations I have used and enjoyed for a *Rapid Bible Read Thru*:

- **New International Version** – This translation is very readable. Without getting into the technicalities of translating philosophies, the NIV is more of a thought-for-thought translation. It is true to the original languages, but puts it into what the translators believe was the original intent. I grew up on the NIV, so it is also the most familiar to me.

- **English Standard Version** – This is becoming more widely popular every year. The ESV is closer to a word-for-word translation. The translators sought to identify what the original text was saying – not just what it meant. I believe this is the best word-for-word translation when it comes to a *combination* of accuracy and readability.

- **New Living Translation** – This translation is another thought-for-thought translation (similar to the NIV). However, it is written at a slightly easier reading level, making it a terrific choice for younger readers, new Christians, or people for whom English is their second language.

- **The Message** – To be clear, this is a paraphrase. I do not recommend it for your first – or even your second – *Rapid Bible Read Thru*. However, after you have done a few, you might want to give *The Message* a try.[3]

What do you think about audio Bibles?

Audio Bibles are a terrific supplement. They are not a good replacement. For some people, having an audio Bible playing while they read a physical Bible helps them focus. For me at least, if I *only* use an audio Bible, I find my mind wandering more – not less.

You might be different. An audio Bible might help you focus. If you are a slow reader, an audio Bible might help you keep a faster pace.

If you have already done a *Rapid Bible Read Thru* or two, an audio Bible could be a fun way to walk through the Bible. Every year, when I invite people to join me for my annual *Rapid Bible Read Thru*, at least a couple people will be using the audio Bible and doing their "reading" during their commute, or on their daily walk.

I should point out one downside of using an audio Bible. If you are using an audio Bible exclusively – and you are driving or exercising while you do it – it will be quite difficult to follow *Guideline 2* (Grab a pen). Make sure you have thought about that and built in time immediately after parking your car or completing your exercise to jot down what you want to remember or share with your partners.

---

3   *If you don't own a Bible, I don't recommend The Message as your one-and-only Bible. I also don't recommend it as a study Bible. The Message is a paraphrase. Think of it as one of your good friends telling you what the Bible says in their own words. Fresh insight…but not suitable for deeper study.*

WHAT IF I FALL BEHIND? DO YOU BUILD IN "CATCH-UP" DAYS?

I have a few answers to this one. The first has to do with positioning yourself to not fall behind in the first place. As you may remember from the chapter on starting well, if you read for an amount of *time* instead of an amount of *content* you will almost always be ahead. That is why I recommend reading for 5-10 minutes longer than is required to finish in the exact amount of time you have committed to.

Another option I have heard people use is to figure out what days in the week will be their longer reading days. For some people, thirty minutes is all they can commit to on work days. Those same people might be able to do an hour or two for the non-work days during the months of the *Rapid Bible Read Thru*.

If you happen to find yourself a little behind, I recommend simply adjusting your reading by 5-10 minutes a day so catching up doesn't feel overwhelming. However, if you get sick or "life happens" early on and you find yourself several days behind, take a look at the week ahead and see if there is a day or two when you can carve out 2-3 hours and catch up then. By the way, many people have told me the days where they sat down for several hours to catch up have been some of the most enjoyable of the entire *Rapid Bible Read Thru*!

WHAT'S A GOOD WAY TO KEEP TRACK OF ITEMS YOU WANT TO RESEARCH LATER?

This one is really a matter of personal preference. Some people like to have a separate notebook (or page in their notebook) for keeping track of sections they want to share with their partners or sections they want to return to after the *Rapid Bible Read Thru* is completed.

One year, I simply kept a single sheet of paper in my Bible and wrote down the Scripture references I wanted to return to. I spent the month or two after the *Rapid Bible Read Thru* looking back at these references. It has been so rewarding, I have continued the practice of devoting one or two months after the *Rapid Bible Read Thru* to revisiting my notes, thoughts, and prayers.

In the last few years, I have been using highlights, tags, or even capital letters in brackets in my digital notebook. Some notes are just for me. I will highlight passages I know I want to discuss with my partners. If there's something I want to dive into later, internalize, record a video about, or write a blog post on, I will simply put [RESEARCH], [INTERNALIZE], [VIDEO], or [BLOG]. That makes is very easy to scan later.

What's the best way to retain gains after the RBRT?

As I mentioned in the last question, most years I spend the month – sometimes two – after the *Rapid Bible Read Thru* walking through the notes I took. I follow up on questions, do some deep study of sections or people, internalize parts, or simply pray through others.

If your group is up for continuing to meet, it would be very helpful to revisit these topics with them. Pick a topic or two to research together. Have each person come with a question or verse to discuss. It will lead to some fantastic discussions.

What works best as far as order of books or does it make any difference?

Personally, I have done a *Rapid Bible Read Thru* using three different approaches. One is reading straight through – Genesis to Revelation. This option works best if you already have a fairly decent handle on the storyline of Scripture.

If you are new to the Bible – or need a refresher on what-happened-and-in-what-order – then I would strongly urge you to go with a chronological reading plan.[4] There are also chronological plans online or even print Bibles that are organized chronologically. Tom, one of the guys in my first group, bought one of these for his second *Rapid Bible Read Thru* and absolutely loved it.

A third option is to choose one of the first two, but add a little twist. Pull out Psalms and Proverbs and read a few *at a different time from the rest of your reading*. I mentioned that I do my reading early in the morning (before the rest of *The Ferrin 5* wakes up and craziness ensues).

---

4   *You can download a printable version for free at* *KeithFerrin.com/chronological*.

This is a really neat way to experience Psalms and Proverbs.[5] Since they are both stylistically poetic, it is nice to simply "soak" in a few at a time. This also helps if you find yourself with some time constraints. Reading Psalms and Proverbs for ten minutes at night provides the opportunity to read for 30-40 minutes in the morning – rather than 45-60 – and still complete the *Rapid Bible Read Thru* in about four months.

WHAT ADVICE WOULD YOU GIVE TO SOMEONE WHO HAS STARTED TO READ THE BIBLE MULTIPLE TIMES, BUT HASN'T FINISHED?

Pray and find some partners. That may sound overly simple, but these are the two most effective strategies if you want to finish this time.

We must always keep in mind that there is a spiritual battle going on *any time* we pick up our Bibles. I have said it before, but it warrants repetition: The enemy does not want you to read, know, enjoy, and apply God's Word. After all, the Word is the Holy Spirit's offensive weapon (Ephesians 6). Satan wants to stop you from ever picking up the Sword. He knows it is much easier to fight someone who isn't carrying a weapon! Pray, my friend. Often.

Let me ask you something. The times when you started, but didn't finish, were you meeting with anyone who was also reading? I am sure it has happened to someone, but as I write this, I can't think of a single person who has started a *Rapid Bible Read Thru* with at least one partner and didn't complete it.

We need accountability. All of us do. And by the way, sometimes it is your partner who needs the accountability. Maybe you are the one encouraging him to keep going. Maybe you are the one who reminds her that you are praying for her and you are in this battle together.

HOW DO I DO THIS IF I'M REALLY BUSY?

This question comes up a lot. Not to trivialize it, but do you know many people who *aren't* busy? Ever since I started my first *Rapid Bible Read Thru* in 2010, I have never heard anyone say, "Sure. That sounds

---

5   *I wouldn't recommend always doing it this way. While it is a nice way to change things up, it's also pretty neat to read Psalms and Proverbs at the same time you are reading the narrative portion of the lives of David, Solomon, etc.*

great. I just had an hour a day open up in my schedule and I was wondering what to fill it with."

Ok...enough with the snarkiness. Now some practical advice.

Completing a *Rapid Bible Read Thru* will cost you something. Something will have to go. When I ask people about this topic as they are doing a *Rapid Bible Read Thru*, I find almost everyone reduces one of three things: sleep, television, or social media.

Take a quick, honest assessment of how much you are sleeping, watching TV, or browsing Facebook, Twitter, or Pinterest (just to name a few). Frequently, people who are super busy don't sleep as much as they need to. If you are in that camp, I don't recommend cutting out even more sleep.

However, I meet very few busy people who haven't been on social media or turned their television on in the last few weeks. I don't know about you, but this quote from Stephen Covey hits a little too close to home,

> "We make time for what is important and
> we make excuses for the rest."

Ouch. True...but ouch!

Decide before you start what you are going to cut out. Habits are strong magnets. If you don't decide and commit to exactly what you will give up, your busyness will likely pull you into the same habits you have always had.

I TRAVEL A LOT. ANY RECOMMENDATIONS FOR ME?

I feel your pain. I am actually typing these words at 35,000 feet! Travel makes consistency hard. Period.

A few recommendations. First, if your travel is routine enough where you *can* build consistency into your travel schedule, that's your best bet.

If not, figure out the blocks of time that are filled with non-essential activities. If you are on an airplane for several hours each week, make "plane time" your "Bible reading time." Leave the TV off at the hotel for the next several months. If you end up eating alone at restaurants, bring your Bible with you.

Is your travel seasonal? If you have busy travel seasons and slower home seasons, I recommend planning your *Rapid Bible Read Thru* for one of your home seasons. It is nice to do it – especially your first one

– at a time when you can commit to a consistent time of day.

Finally, if you were planning on a four-month timeframe, you could go with six months to shave some time off the daily reading. Thirty minutes a day will get you there pretty easily.

Should I read all at once or break it into small chunks throughout the day?

There is no doubt in my mind that you are significantly more likely to succeed – and enjoy it more! – if you figure out one, consistent time each day where you can read for an extended period of time. I have certainly known people who have read in smaller chunks throughout the day. However, I have known way more people who have tried that approach and *not* finished, than people who have.

If your schedule simply will not allow you to commit a 30-minute block of time, make sure that each of your reading times are at least fifteen or twenty minutes. As I mentioned earlier, our brains don't really kick in until the 10-minute mark. Trying to read 5-10 minutes here or there will never have you engaged in God's Word in a way that will help you enjoy and remember what you read. (And that's kind of important, wouldn't you say?)

What do I do when what I am reading is difficult to understand?

In those situations, jot a quick note so you can return to it later. Many times, as you keep reading and get the context, the question you have will get answered. Other times, it won't.

Bringing those questions to your group is often helpful. Otherwise, when your *Rapid Bible Read Thru* is completed, you will likely have several questions, people, or passages you will want to return to. That is the time to dive deep into those sections in your notes.

Is it ok to skim some sections?

Yes. While you might have just cringed, if you are reading this answer, my guess is it's more likely you breathed a sigh of relief. One of the main reasons for doing a *Rapid Bible Read Thru* is to immerse yourself in the narrative of the Bible. Sometimes, skimming a long list of names (see Numbers) or laws (see Leviticus) actually *helps* you stay in the narrative, while reading every word *hinders* you.

Please don't hear what I am not saying. I am *not* saying there is no value in the names, laws, or the detailed description of the temple. I am *not* saying you should skim them every time. I am *not* saying these details can't be awe-inspiring, informative, or draw you closer to the heart of the Father. They absolutely can.

You should read them. That doesn't mean you have to read them *every* time. If your goal is to get the Big Picture of the Bible, you might want to skim a few parts. Let me put it this way: I would rather have you skim a few parts and enjoy reading the Bible, rather than reading every word and quitting in the middle – or possibly even worse – finishing out of a sense of obligation. God loves you. Time in His Word is time hanging out with Him.

Amen?

PART 3

HOW DO I HOST A *RAPID BIBLE READ THRU*?

The Best Option

As I mentioned in the chapter *Keep the Process Simple*, Guideline 3 is "Find a Few Partners." Obviously, since you are reading this chapter on hosting a *Rapid Bible Read Thru*, you are taking that guideline seriously. (Well done, my friend.)

Before getting too far, I want to assuage any concerns that well up inside you when you hear the word "hosting." You might have visions of a weekly commitment to making your house spotless, providing coffee served in matching mugs, and warm scones with raspberry jam.[1]

That is *not* what I am talking about here.

When it comes to hosting a *Rapid Bible Read Thru*, it is basically about getting the group started, keeping the conversation rolling, and sending out reminders or changes as needed.

Meet Face-to-Face

There is nothing like sitting in a room with someone face-to-face. (Preferably with coffee.) To be able to look into each other's eyes. To hear the intonation in a question. To see the body language. To hear the laughter.

Yes. Getting together in the same physical location is, by far, the best option. Sometimes it's not possible. But if it is, do it.

---

1   While the rest of this chapter is about how to "simply" host a Rapid Bible Read Thru, *if you do decide to host one with coffee and warm scones with raspberry jam, send me the invite. I'm not one to turn down either of those.*

FIND THE RIGHT PEOPLE.

If you are the host, figure out whom you want to do the *Rapid Bible Read Thru* with. Ask yourself a few questions like...

- Is this just for men, just for women, or a mix?
- Are couples doing this together?
- Do we want to be intentional about having an inter-generational group?
- Do I want to find 5-8 people or one other really committed person?
- Do I want to do this primarily with other Christians or as a way to introduce someone to the Bible – and Jesus Himself?
- Is there someone in my life – at church, work, neighborhood, etc. – whom God is leading me to invite?

The answers to these questions will guide both whom you invite, where you meet, and how you facilitate the conversation.

PICK THE RIGHT TIME AND LOCATION

After you have made the invitations and received an overwhelming "Yes!" from each one (a man can dream, right?) now is the time to settle on the when and where.

Picking the right time and location is all about picking the right time and location *for your group*. Some groups are meeting before work, so picking a centrally-located coffee shop is ideal. Other groups plan to add time for sharing and praying together. In that case, a coffee shop might not be your best bet.

If your group happens to attend the same church, maybe you could meet right before or after church. Or even grab some lunch after church. If your group consists of parents of teenagers, you could meet in a room at the church – or a nearby restaurant or ice cream shop – while the kids are at youth group.

Think of the timing, location, and personalities in your group. Then pick a time and location that fits all of you. One big mistake people make is to decide on the when and where first. You would hate to have someone decline the invitation simply because the time or location doesn't work!

KEEP THE CONVERSATION MOVING

This one is also going to be determined quite a bit by the people who make up your group. For most groups, it can be as simple as having people share the answer to this question:

What conversations did you have with God
as you read the Bible this week?

These "conversations" will lead to insights, struggles, questions, applications, and a whole host of other topics.

It is important to keep in mind that, as the host, you are *not* leading a Bible study. A Bible study is not the same thing as a *Rapid Bible Read Thru*. You are not the teacher. You are not the one who "has all the right answers."

It is important for the group to know that. And it is important for *you* to know that. This is especially tricky if you have lead a lot of Bible studies or taught Sunday School classes in the past.

Most of your "hosting duties" are done before and after the time your group is actually together. You are the organizer. You are the reminder (if needed). You are the encourager.

When you are actually together, you simply want to make sure everyone has the opportunity to share – and is encouraged to do so!

This is even more important if your group is made up of long-time Bible readers as well as new believers or people simply exploring the Bible or faith for the first time. In those cases, do everything you can to keep the conversation free of church lingo. The last thing you want is for someone to feel like they needed to already know the Bible in order to read the Bible.

ONE FINAL NOTE

As the host, sometimes you need to have the boldness to initiate the hard conversation with someone in the group who is dominating the conversation. This isn't the place to get into the art and science of conflict resolution. So let me simply provide a couple suggestions.

First, set the expectations at the first gathering. Remind *everyone* that no one is the teacher. No one is the student. No one is the talker. Everyone shares. Everyone asks. Everyone answers. Everyone is valued.

Setting expectations at the very first gathering will go a long way toward making your *Rapid Bible Read Thru* a huge success. When the expectations are clear, you can point back to the expectations and purpose of the group, rather than having it feel like a personal attack.

Address *general* guidance to the whole group, and *specific* guidance in private. Oftentimes, when one person is talking more than they should, it is enough to simply remind the group (at the beginning of the next gathering) that "We want everyone to have a chance to share. So please keep that in mind as your share your thoughts, insights, and questions."

However, we know that some people won't get the hint. (Insert heavy sigh here.) In those cases, it will be necessary to talk to the person between gatherings. Remind them of the difference between a *Rapid Bible Read Thru* and a Bible study. Remind them of the desire to hear from everyone. Remind them that you want to hear from them!

Find the right people. Decide on the when and where. Keep the conversation moving. It truly doesn't need to get more complicated than that.

The Two Next-Best Options

As much as you might want to get together in person, sometimes it just doesn't work out. Your work schedule might not allow for an in-person get together at the same time each week. Or maybe you really want to do a *Rapid Bible Read Thru* with people who live in different cities, states, or countries. Or maybe you put a valiant effort into hosting a group and simply can't find anyone local who is ready or willing to jump on board.

Whatever the reason, please hear this clearly: You will still benefit greatly from having someone – even if they live far away – who is doing the *Rapid Bible Read Thru* with you.

I am sure there are several options other than the ones I will mention in the paragraphs that follow. These are the ones I have used – or heard about others using – with great success (and ease). By the way, I am referring to these as the "two next-best options" rather than ranking them because they both have their benefits and drawbacks.

Start a Private Facebook Group

Are you on Facebook? Are the people you'll be doing the *Rapid Bible Read Thru* with on Facebook.

Yup. That's what I thought.

Almost everyone is on Facebook. And starting a private Facebook group *literally* takes less than five minutes (and that's generous).

Things may change (Facebook likes to change things just for fun), but for the last couple years, creating a private Facebook group goes something like this…

1. Go to your News Feed on Facebook.

2. In the left column, you'll see Favorites, then Pages, then Groups. (There are other categories as you scroll down, but Groups is where you want to be.)

3. The last item under Groups is "Create Group."

4. Click that and a little window pops up that is as easy as filling out a form.

5. Name the group.

6. Invite members (start typing their names and it will autofill).

7. Click "Secret."

8. Click "Create."

That's it. Of course, if you *want* to add an image to the top or a description, you're free to do that. But you can complete those five steps in less than two minutes.

One quick side note: Let's say you happen to find someone who wants to participate and is *not* on Facebook. Gasp! They can still participate in your Facebook group. On the popup form where you create the group and invite people to join, if you enter an email address instead of a name, it will send people an invitation. They can join Facebook, but do nothing other than participate in your group.

As you have heard me mention, I not only have a small, in-person group I meet with. I also invite my blog readers to join me in a private Facebook group I create every year.

There are so many cool things about this group. People share insights on a daily basis. Questions get asked and answered. Resources are shared. You can record a video with your phone and post it *only* to the group.

In case you are concerned about something getting shared (intentionally or accidentally) with the whole Facebook universe, no need. When you post something in a private group, the only buttons available are "Like" and "Comment." The "Share" button isn't even an option. Lovely.

You can also upload files or photos that only the group can see. For example, let's say you find a really cool infographic on the life of David, a map of Paul's missionary journeys, or a PDF of the chronological plan you are using. Simply upload it using the "Photos" or "Files" buttons at the top of the group page and everyone has access to see, comment, or download them for their own use.

There are lots of aspects about a private Facebook group that I love. The one aspect I less-than-love is the fact that while the sharing, commenting, replying, and liking are *interactive* – they are not *immediate*. It is one thing to post a thought and have people comment. It is a very different thing altogether to share a thought and have a face-to-face conversation at a coffee shop or in a living room.

GET TOGETHER USING A VIDEO OR AUDIO CONFERENCE CALL

If location is your primary barrier, setting up a consistent, weekly video or audio conference is a terrific option. And believe it or not, it's free and way easier than you would think.

While it's still not as good as sitting a room with a few friends, video or audio conferencing is certainly an amazing way to see and hear from people who don't live anywhere near you.

Here are my three favorite video tools and my favorite audio tool. (All are free, by the way.)

SKYPE

Skype is getting better and better. Most people have an account already. If you have a computer or a smartphone, you can get it for free. It used to be that you had to pay for a premium account to use Skype with more than one person. That's not the case anymore. Now you can have up to ten with a standard, free account.[1] Everyone can see everyone else at the same time.

GOOGLE HANGOUTS

While I prefer Skype, Google Hangouts might be a better option if everyone is a regular Gmail user. Some people have told me the video and audio quality is a bit better with Google Hangouts, though I haven't experienced a lot of differences between the two.

Since you need to have a Gmail account to start a Hangout, that puts a limit on you if the person with the Gmail account misses a week. It used to be that everyone on the Hangout had to be a Gmail

---

1   *If it all possible, you'll want to have everyone hard-wired into their internet connection, rather than using Wi-Fi. Video takes a lot of bandwidth, and video conferencing with more than one person will put a strain on any coffee shop Wi-Fi connection.*

user. That's not the case anymore. The person with the Gmail account creates the Hangout and invites everyone else via email. The recipients simply need to click the link.

Zoom

I saved the least-known (and yet my personal favorite) for last. Like the other two, Zoom is free. Create an account at Zoom.us and you're ready to go.

Experientially, once you're on the video call, it works pretty much the same as Skype and Google Hangouts. However, there are three really cool differences.

First, the quality is terrific! I use Zoom for meetings, interviews, etc. I have rarely ever had any quality issues with video or audio quality. It just works.

Second, scheduling the calls is super easy. If the people in your group use electronic calendars (Google, Outlook, iCalendar, etc.) one of you simply creates a "meeting." Everyone is emailed the details. You can set a reminder like with any other meeting. And when it comes time for your group to meet, simply click the link in the meeting request. Love it.

Third, you can record it. If one of your group members is going to miss a week, hit record and the video and audio will be recorded and saved on your computer. If you're also using the private Facebook group, you can upload it there.[2]

FreeConferenceCall

If you prefer audio only, this is the best option I have found. Head on over to FreeConferenceCall.com and sign up for an account. Like the others, it's free.

It works like any other conference call provider. As the host, you have a web interface for starting the calls and a special Host ID number than identifies you as the host.

You simply give your group members the phone number to call and the Participant ID (same for everyone). They call in, enter in the Participant ID and you're all connected.

As with Zoom, FCC has very good quality. I haven't had any issues at all. Also like Zoom, it has the ability to record. However, with

2   *As of this writing, Zoom only allows for 40 minutes of recording (per meeting) with the free account.*

FCC, it's even simpler. The recording has a 6-hour time limit, so I'm guessing that won't be a problem. It also records onto *their server*.

When it's all said and done, you have the option of downloading the audio file or simply sending everyone a link. You can even password-protect the link, so only your members can access the recording. Very cool.

I'll Take the Combo, Please!

Whether you use Skype, Google Hangouts, Zoom, or FreeConferenceCall, I highly recommend you *also* setup a private Facebook group. The combined benefits of consistent conversations, as well as the ability to share thoughts, questions, photos, and resources whenever you have the chance, will provide you with an experience much closer to the benefits of getting together.

Bottom line: If you can get together…do it. If you can't…set up a private Facebook group and a video or audio conference call.

What Are the Most Common Questions about HOSTING a Rapid Bible Read Thru?

You might be tired of hearing this, but doing a *Rapid Bible Read Thru* is way more beneficial – not to mention a lot more fun! – when you do it with others. I say it a lot because again and again, when people tell me they didn't complete a *Rapid Bible Read Thru* or got to the point where it was task or chore each day, I ask them if they were getting together with others.

I have *never* heard someone who didn't finish or didn't enjoy it who answered "Yes" to that question. Never.

For any group of people to get together regularly, someone has to be the host. (Feel free to use the word *organizer, facilitator,* or *detail-person-who-likes-to-send-out-the-emails* if you like those words better than *host.*)

As with the chapter at the end of *Part 2*, this chapter is written to be scanned rather than read straight through. Look through the questions and see if any of them match questions you have. In general, I have arranged the questions in this basic order: Getting Started, During the *Rapid Bible Read Thru*, and Miscellaneous.

My guess is, your question will be answered in the next few pages. If not, shoot me an email or ask a question on my Facebook Page[1]. Check out the "Let's Connect" page at the end of the book for several ways to contact me.

---

1   *I regularly interact with readers on my Facebook Page:* Facebook.com/KeithFerrin.

IS IT BEST TO START WITH A GROUP YOU ALREADY HAVE SUCH AS SUNDAY SCHOOL CLASS OR START A COMPLETELY NEW GROUP?

In most situations, it is actually best to start with a new group. The main reason is to avoid the "awkwardness" factor. A *Rapid Bible Read Thru* does require an increased – though doable – level of commitment. Not everyone in your Sunday School class (or small group or youth group or Bible study) may want – or have the time – to commit to that. Rather than say the awkward "No," most people will say "Yes" so they don't disappoint the group. However, those people rarely follow through and either end up way behind (awkward), begin making excuses to miss the get together (awkward), or drop out of the group altogether after a month or two (awkward and sad).

Another reason starting a new group is beneficial is it makes it a special thing. With a new group, a starting date, and a target ending date, there will be more excitement and follow-through for those who commit. With the new group – started specifically for the *Rapid Bible Read Thru* – there will be no expectation of this being an ongoing group. Hopefully, some of the people in your group will go on to host a *Rapid Bible Read Thru* of their own!

HOW DO I MAKE IT APPEALING TO OTHERS?

I will answer the question with another question: Have you done a *Rapid Bible Read Thru* before? If so, the best way to make it appealing is to simply share your experience. What was your experience? How did your relationship with God change and grow during that time? What did you learn? How has it impacted your thinking about and understanding of the Bible?

If you haven't done a *Rapid Bible Read Thru* yourself, the best approach is one of "Let's go on this journey together." Everyone loves an adventure. Everyone loves it more if they go on an adventure with a partner (or several).

One thing I would *not* do is make the invitation primarily about "Bible knowledge." Information is not motivation. Transformation is motivation.

When is the best time to meet?

Each year, our group has met in the early morning on a weekday. That seems to be the time when most people can carve out a *consistent* time. That said, if you all attend the same church, it might be a perfect fit to start a new group and meet during the hour before or after church. I have heard of Saturday morning groups or even weekday evenings.

One other suggestion: Once you get a couple commitments, land on a time before inviting too many more people. It is easier to add people to an existing day, time, and location, than to invite six to eight people and then try to figure out a time that works for everyone. Possible. But difficult.

What do we do when group members are in different time zones?

From a logistics standpoint, you will likely need to have fewer people in the group if you're going across multiple time zones. Finding a consistent day and time is hard enough with people in the same time zone. Adding one or two more time zones increases that challenge. Again, just because it is difficult doesn't mean it is not worth it!

How do I stop it from being an in-depth Bible study?

This is all about setting expectations the very first time you get together. Making it clear that this is *not* an in-depth study. The purpose is to read, notice, and share. The purpose is not analysis, explanation, and providing answers.

If your group is made up of people who have participated in lots of Bible studies, this will likely be a shift (and a challenge) for them. Some groups have found it helpful to set a five-minute timer so each person can share. No comments. No this-is-what-I-think-that-section-means. After everyone has had a chance to share, you can either go around again or open it up to a more general discussion.

WHAT'S THE EASIEST WAY TO COMMUNICATE WITH THE GROUP?

The two ways I have communicated with the group more than anything else are email and a private Facebook group.[2] They are simple. Almost everyone has both. People already know how to use them. And neither requires an immediate response.

There are certainly several other ways groups could communicate. I have heard about a group that texted each other verses, insights, or questions throughout the week. One person I know started a "group" with one other guy. They had quick "check in" calls a couple times a week. You could also snap a picture of your Bible and send the picture to someone in your group via text, Instagram, or Snapchat.[3]

HOW DO I ENCOURAGE SOMEONE WHO FEELS EMBARRASSED OR INADEQUATE IN THEIR KNOWLEDGE OF THE BIBLE?

Remind them there will not be a test – weekly or when you finish. This is designed to be an enjoyable discussion, not a time focused on learning and knowledge. Invite them to jot down their questions for sure, but make it clear that what they know or don't know is not the point. Conversations with God each day – and with each other when you meet – is the point.

WHAT IF MY GROUP IS MOSTLY NEW – OR NOT YET – CHRISTIANS?

In general, I would give the same answer as I did in the previous question. However, I would also add one thing. If someone is brand new to faith in Jesus (or simply exploring), I would think through whether a *Rapid Bible Read Thru* is the right place to start.

It might be. Or, it might be best to start with Matthew, Mark, Luke, John, and Acts. That way, they get a really good look at the life of Jesus. Who He was, what He did, how He lived, and how His

---

2   *See the previous chapter for step-by-step details on how to create a private Facebook group.*

3   *Those last three suggestions were for the benefit of my middle schoolers and their friends. I think they both just smiled and sighed at the same time.*

early followers lived and spread the good news.[4] After that, you can do a *Rapid Bible Read Thru* with those who are interested in the next step.

SHOULD EVERYONE BE READING IN THE SAME TRANSLATION?

No. (How's that for a short answer?)

I have done a *Rapid Bible Read Thru* in several translations now. I have never had a time when we were all reading the same translation. Having different people reading different translations is actually helpful. It adds another "voice" to the conversation.

In case you didn't read the question about translations in the Q & A chapter at the end of Part 2, here are my four favorite translations:

- **New International Version** – This translation is very readable. Without getting into the technicalities of translating philosophies, the NIV is more of a thought-for-thought translation. It is true to the original languages, but puts it into what the translators believe was the original intent. I grew up on the NIV, so it is also the most familiar to me.

- **English Standard Version** – This is becoming more widely popular every year. The ESV is closer to a word-for-word translation. The translators sought to identify what the original text was saying – not just what it meant. I believe this is the best word-for-word translation when it comes to a *combination* of accuracy and readability.

- **New Living Translation** – This translation is another thought-for-thought translation (similar to the NIV). However, it is written at a slightly lower grade level, making it a terrific choice for younger readers, new Christians, or people for whom English is their second language.

- **The Message** – To be clear, this is a paraphrase. I do not recommend it for your first – or even your second – *Rapid*

---

4   *I go into a lot more detail about this in Tip 9 of my book* How to Enjoy Reading Your Bible. *Of all the books I've written, that's the one I give away to new/young/not-yet believers.*

Bible Read Thru. However, after you have done a few, you might want to give *The Message* a try.[5]

How do I encourage group members during the *Rapid Bible Read Thru* (without being a pest)?

Honestly, the best way to encourage group members is to consistently show up to the weekly conversation with a listening ear. Let them share what they are seeing, what they are learning, and what confuses them.

If you start a private Facebook group, contribute a few times a week. Send them a text or give them a call now and then.

Make sure you don't overdo it. I have actually found that people don't need much encouragement once they get started. Getting together and talking about the Bible covers most of the encouragement people need.

What is the best way to maintain accountability?

This goes hand-in-hand with the last question. Don't overdo it. Most people don't need – or want – the accountability. The weekly get together is the accountability.

At the first gathering, it might be helpful to ask if anyone wants or needs accountability and how often they want it. I heard about a group that would text each other their favorite verse for the day. This added a sense of fun and connection on a daily basis. It also certainly built in the accountability since everyone was expecting to hear from everyone else each day!

Can a *Rapid Bible Read Thru* work for a whole church?

Yes…But…

---

5   *If you don't own a Bible, I <u>don't</u> recommend* The Message *as your one-and-only Bible. I also don't recommend it as a study Bible. It is a paraphrase. Think of it as one of your good friends telling you what the Bible says in their own words. Fresh insight…but not suitable for deeper study.*

Yes, it can work. Yes, it can be life-changing for those who participate. Yes, it can be transformational for a church community intentionally soaking in the Word together.

But, it is rare that you'll get a large number of people to participate, so you need to be okay with that. But, it's going to take promotion, coordination, and invitation to make sure those who jump on board are also plugged into a weekly group that meets at a time and place that consistently works for them. Yes…you should do it. But…be prepared to do some extra legwork.

HOW KNOWLEDGEABLE DO I HAVE TO BE TO HOST A RBRT?

If you can invite people, you are knowledgeable enough. Remember, you are not teaching a class on the multiple theological viewpoints found in the Book of Revelation. You are hosting a discussion of people who are reading the Bible and talking about it.

The only exception I would make is that if you are purposefully building a group of people who are very new to faith and the Bible, it would be helpful to have someone in the group (if it's not you) who can answer some of the basic questions that will surely get asked.

WHAT WORKS FOR DIFFERENT AGES?

The biggest challenge with multiple ages tends to be scheduling the gatherings. That said, groups with people of different generations lead to fantastic conversations!

Specifically for younger people (teens and twenties), I find that meeting weekly – and in person – is almost always necessary for consistency and completion. For people older than that, weekly is still ideal, but every-other-week can still work. For some reason, with school, sports, young families, new jobs, etc. not having a gathering every week will quickly turn into not showing up at all.

WHAT ARE COMMON MISTAKES OF HOSTING A *RAPID BIBLE READ THRU*?

This may sound over-simplified, but the biggest mistake you can make is not starting a group. You may think you're not Bible-smart enough. Yes, you are. You may think you don't have the time. Yes, you do. You may think you're not the "hosting type." If you can read, have a conversation, and send someone directions to a nearby coffee shop, you're a host.

Start a group. A few months from now you – and the people you invite – will be really glad you did.

The Final Question...

There you have it. My experience, thoughts, ideas, tips, and encouragement for the "Why" and "How" of doing and hosting a *Rapid Bible Read Thru*. Before I completely wrap this thing up – and you get started reading – I want to answer one question I haven't answered yet.

What do I do after I have completed my *Rapid Bible Read Thru*?

As I told you in the "My Story" chapter, doing a *Rapid Bible Read Thru* has become an annual practice for me. Many people have told me they have started doing the same. Each year, the experience is richer than the year before.

However, since I do my *Rapid Bible Read Thru* in four months each year, that leaves eight more months. There was one year where I did three back-to-back *Rapid Bible Read Thrus,* but every other year I have only done one.

The answer to the question isn't as specific as you may think (or hope). The Bible is so rich and alive, there are many ways to keep learning, growing, and enjoying the Bible.

Here are a few suggestions:

1. Spend a month or two slowly walking through the notes you took during your *Rapid Bible Read Thru*.

2. Focus on the life of Jesus by reading – and rereading – the gospels (Matthew, Mark, Luke, and John)

3. Pick a person from the Bible (Paul, Moses, Peter, David, etc.) and read all the parts of the Bible that are either about them or written by them.

4. Pick a "category" of people (Bible authors, women, writers of different Psalms, kings of Israel and Judah, Paul's traveling companions, etc.) and explore as much as you can about the people in those categories.

5. Pick a short book of the Bible and hunker down for a couple months.[1] (This one is my favorite.)

Whatever you choose to do – make sure you choose something! Many times, I have heard about people who "take a week or two off" after completing a *Rapid Bible Read Thru*.

This is a really bad decision.

Hopefully the *Rapid Bible Read Thru* has developed in you a hunger for God and His Word. Feed that hunger! After all, while you and I both like a variety in the meals we eat, I am guessing you never "took a week or two off" from eating!

Variety is fine. In fact, it is necessary! But when it comes to Bible reading being integrated into your daily life, taking a week or two off will frequently lead to a month or two.

---

1   *I highly recommend doing this with at least one or two books of the Bible every year. My first book –* Falling In Love with God's Word *– is entirely devoted to my process of studying a book of the Bible.*

MAY I PRAY FOR YOU?

Rather than come up with some witty final paragraph, let's do something really valuable. Let's pray.

Father God, I thank you for the opportunity to share these words with the person holding this book. I pray You would develop in them a deep love for You as they read Your Word. Foster a genuine wonder, a greater understanding, and an authentic enjoyment of the Bible. Whether they are doing their very first Rapid Bible Read Thru, hosting a group for the first time, or walking through the Bible for the tenth time, give them fresh insight, transformational application, and a reminder of Your Presence as they read. May their reading, their prayers, and their discussions lead them daily and forever back to You.

By the power of Your Spirit and in the beautiful name of Your Son Jesus Christ, I pray all of this. To You be the glory – forever and ever.

Amen.

ABOUT THE AUTHOR

Am I the only one who thinks it is a little bit strange that the "About the Author" page is typically the only page in an entire book written in the third person? After all, I am the author. I am writing this page. It feels a bit weird to write about myself in the third person.

So let's try this...

I, Keith Ferrin, am an author, speaker, storyteller, and blogger. Actually, that's more of what I "do." As far as who I am...I am a disciple of Jesus Christ, a husband to Kari (world's most outstanding wife), and a father to Sarah, Caleb, and Hannah (the three coolest – and craziest – kids on the planet).

In case you are still reading...I am also a coffee drinker, ice cream eater, youth soccer coach (who occasionally makes the mistake of thinking my body can still do what it did when I was 17), amateur guitar player, lover of twisty-turny movies, and eater of almost any kind of food (except olives).

If you're looking for me, head on up to Seattle. I will be the happy guy hanging out with his wife and kids doing something outside. Unless, of course, it is family movie night. Then we'll be inside.

Let's Connect

I love to connect with my readers. Truly. Shoot me an email. I'll write back.

There are lots of ways we can connect. Here are a few:

- Email: keith@KeithFerrin.com
- Blog: KeithFerrin.com
- Twitter (@KeithFerrin)
- Facebook (Facebook.com/KeithFerrin)
- Pinterest (Pinterest.com/KeithFerrin)
- Instagram (@KeithFerrin)
- Google+ (@KeithFerrin)

And if you have a question, comment, or idea for another book, or a topic you'd like me to write about on the blog, please shoot me a note.

I'd love to hear from you.

Alongside,

Keith

HOW TO ENJOY READING YOUR BIBLE

Do you *enjoy* the Bible? If we enjoy the Bible, we will read it. If we enjoy it, we'll talk about it. If we enjoy it, consistency won't be a problem. After almost two decades of speaking and writing, I have compiled my "Top 10 Tips" for enjoying the Bible. Tips that are applicable immediately. Written using stories, analogies, and common language, these tips are equally accessible for someone who is exploring, is new to faith in Jesus, or has been hanging out with Jesus for decades. If you want to *enjoy* the Bible – I wrote this book for you. Because believing it's true is not enough.

LIKE ICE CREAM: THE SCOOP ON HELPING THE NEXT GENERATION FALL IN LOVE WITH GOD'S WORD

What if passing on a love for God's Word could be as natural – and enjoyable – as passing on a love for ice cream? I believe it can be. When it comes to helping the next generation fall in love with the Bible, the principles are surprisingly similar to the way a love for ice cream gets passed on from generation to generation. Whether you are a parent, grandparent, youth pastor – or anyone who cares deeply about the next generation – you will find *Like Ice Cream* filled with encouragement and practical ideas you can start using today.

FALLING IN LOVE WITH GOD'S WORD

This book will help you discover what God always intended Bible study to be. God wants you to understand His Word. He wants you to enjoy your time in His Word. He wants you to remember what you read in His Word. In this book, I walk you through my entire process of Bible study and Scripture Internalization. My prayer is this book will transform your Bible study time in a way that will allow God to use His Word to transform you!

LOTS OF FREE eBOOKS AT KEITHFERRIN.COM

Here are a few...

- The Christian Parent's Toolbox
- My Top 10 Online Bible Study Tools
- 49 Identity Messages Your Kids Need to Know
- 6 Tips for a Distraction-Free Quiet Time
- 5 Simple Ways to Help Your Kids Know – and Enjoy – the Bible

RAPID BIBLE READ THRU
NOTES

Date:

RBRT Participants:

Notes:

DATE:

RBRT PARTICIPANTS:

NOTES:

Date:

RBRT Participants:

Notes:

Date:

RBRT Participants:

Notes:

DATE:

RBRT PARTICIPANTS:

NOTES:

DATE:

RBRT PARTICIPANTS:

NOTES:

DATE:

RBRT PARTICIPANTS:

NOTES:

Made in the USA
Middletown, DE
07 July 2021